THIS **OR** THAT? History Edition

Joining the
CALIFORNIA
GOLD RUSH
A This or That Debate

by Jessica Rusick

CAPSTONE PRESS
a capstone imprint

Capstone Captivate is published by Capstone Press, an imprint of Capstone.
1710 Roe Crest Drive
North Mankato, Minnesota 56003
www.capstonepub.com

Library of Congress Cataloging-in-Publication Data is available on the Library of Congress website.
ISBN: 978-1-4966-8392-2 (library binding)
ISBN: 978-1-4966-8790-6 (paperback)
ISBN: 978-1-4966-8443-1 (eBook PDF)

Summary: In 1849, more than 90,000 people traveled to California to mine for gold after it was discovered in a river there the year before. This gold rush boosted California's population and helped it become a state. Test your decision-making skills with this or that questions about joining the gold rush!

Image Credits
iStockphoto: Grafissimo, 27, powerofforever, 12, 18, 26, xavierarnau, 3, ZU_09, 13; Library of Congress: 20, 28; Shutterstock: alicja neumiler, 25, ArtMari, 16, behindlens, 10, Bobkeenan Photography, Cover (Coloma River), chippix, 6, Eifel Kreutz, 15, I. Pilon, Cover (map), iamanewbee, 17, Jairo Rene Leiva, 14, JIANG HONGYAN, 30, josefauer, Cover (pickax), leo_photo, 11, N8Allen, 24, pamas, Cover (gold stones), Robert Gubbins, Cover (gold panning), Stephanie Murton, 23, Sue Leonard Photography, 9, Will Pedro, 29, Yakov Oskanov, 22, Zoran Milic, 5 (map); Wikimedia Commons: 19, 21, J. H. Richardson, 8, Library of Congress, 4–5 (Portsmouth Square), 7

Design Elements: I. Pilon/Shutterstock (background map)

Editorial Credits
Editor: Rebecca Felix; Designers: Aruna Rangarajan & Tamara JM Peterson; Production Specialist: Tori Abraham

All internet sites appearing in back matter were available and accurate when this book was sent to press.

Printed in the United States of America.
PA117

A HUGE DISCOVERY

In January 1848, gold flakes were discovered in a California river. News of the discovery spread across the country and overseas.

In 1849, about 90,000 people traveled to California to mine for gold. These people were called "forty-niners." Many were immigrants from China or Europe. A few became rich. Most did not.

By 1850, surface gold was hard to find. Miners joined mining companies or found new jobs. Some went back home. However, many stayed and made new lives. This new population helped California become a state in 1850.

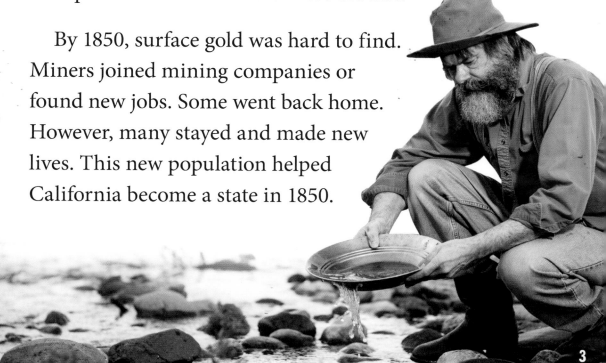

HOW TO USE THIS BOOK

What if you had gone to California during the gold rush? What choices would you have made? Do you think you would have survived?

This book is full of questions that relate to the California gold rush. Some are questions real people had to face.

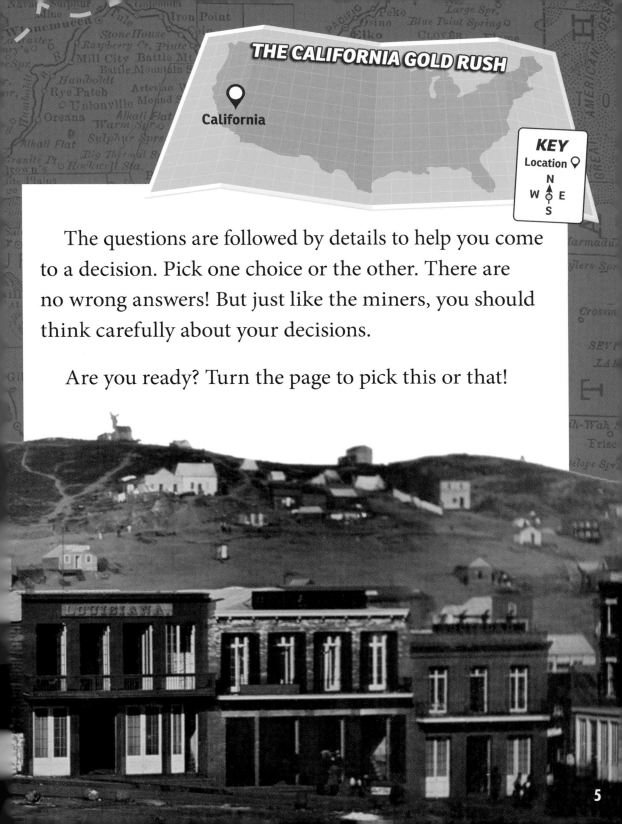

California

KEY

Location

N
W E
S

The questions are followed by details to help you come to a decision. Pick one choice or the other. There are no wrong answers! But just like the miners, you should think carefully about your decisions.

Are you ready? Turn the page to pick this or that!

THIS

To travel to California by **LAND?**

> could involve lots of walking

> encounter many dangerous landscapes

> could become stranded

Some miners used the California Trail to get to California. This was a dirt trail about 2,000 miles (3,219 kilometers) long. Travelers had to guide their wagons across rocks, **ruts**, and deserts. The trail went through two mountain ranges. If travelers didn't time their journeys correctly, they could become stranded in the winter snow.

OR THAT?

To travel to California by WATER?

- don't have to walk as far
- cramped and dirty conditions
- face dangers from jungle

Other miners got to California by boat. Some traveled around the tip of South America on crowded ships. This trip was 14,000 miles (22,500 km) long. Others saved 8,000 miles (12,900 km) by traveling through Panama by river canoe. This route involved a few days' hike through a jungle. After leaving the jungle, miners waited weeks to take another boat to California.

THIS

To sleep in a
TENT?

> easy to put up

> face cold and rain

> not much privacy

Tents allowed miners to stay near where they mined. A tent was quick and affordable housing. It was easy to put up and take down. However, tents didn't provide much protection from rain or cold. Many tents were often crowded together. Miners would also be more exposed to waste from people living in nearby tents.

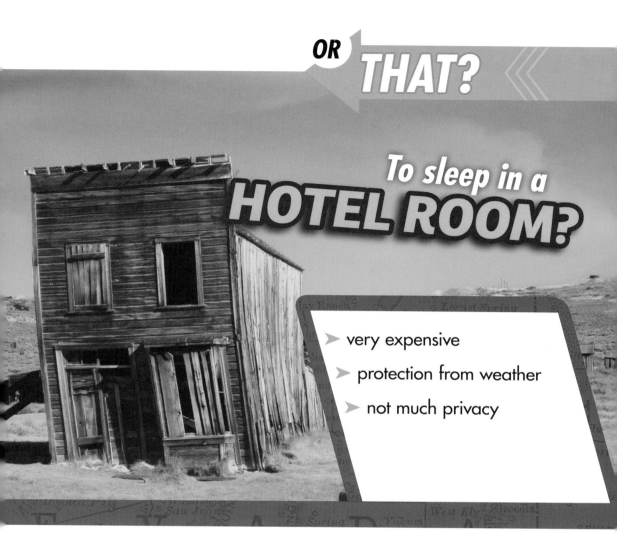

To sleep in a
HOTEL ROOM?

> very expensive

> protection from weather

> not much privacy

Miners could also pay for a hotel room. Rooms were expensive. They could cost up to $2,400 a month. That's about $70,000 in today's money! A room would protect miners from cold and storms. However, a miner would still not have much privacy. Rooms were usually only separated by thin boards or pieces of cloth.

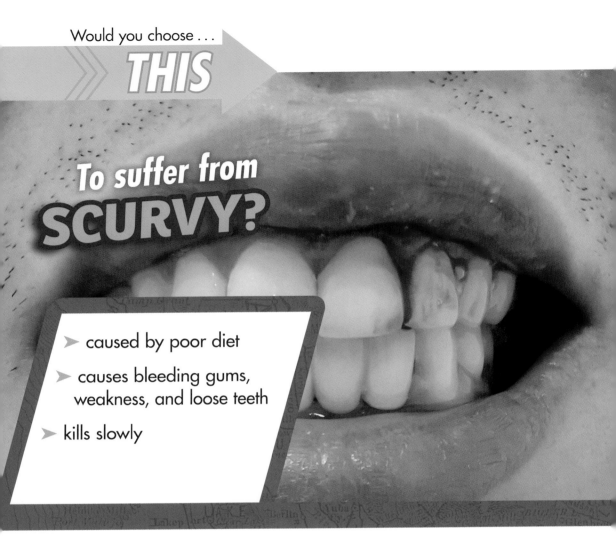

THIS

To suffer from SCURVY?

➤ caused by poor diet

➤ causes bleeding gums, weakness, and loose teeth

➤ kills slowly

Miners did not have much access to fresh fruits and vegetables during the gold rush. These foods have vitamin C. Many miners got scurvy because they did not get enough of this vitamin. Scurvy causes weakness, bleeding gums, loose teeth, and more. It can also cause death over a few months' time.

To suffer from
CHOLERA?

➤ caused by bacteria

➤ vomiting and diarrhea

➤ kills quickly in some cases

Many miners got cholera from drinking filthy water or eating spoiled food. Cholera is caused by a certain kind of **bacteria**. It causes **vomiting** and **diarrhea**. This means the body loses water, which can quickly cause death. Cholera deaths during the gold rush were part of a larger cholera outbreak in the United States. Thousands of people died before and after reaching California.

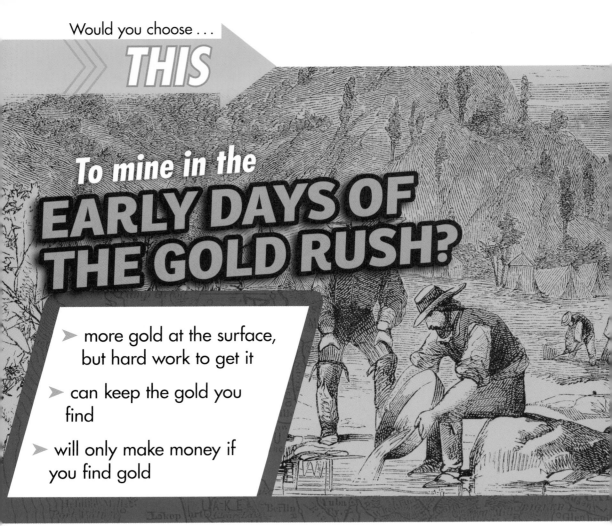

Would you choose . . .

THIS

To mine in the
EARLY DAYS OF THE GOLD RUSH?

➤ more gold at the surface, but hard work to get it

➤ can keep the gold you find

➤ will only make money if you find gold

Early miners found gold at the surface by **panning** in rivers. This involved standing in cold water and swirling dirt in a pan. Miners worked alone or in small groups. They kept the gold they found. Miners could "strike it rich" by finding a lot of gold. However, they could go into debt if they didn't find gold. They still had to spend money on mining equipment and food.

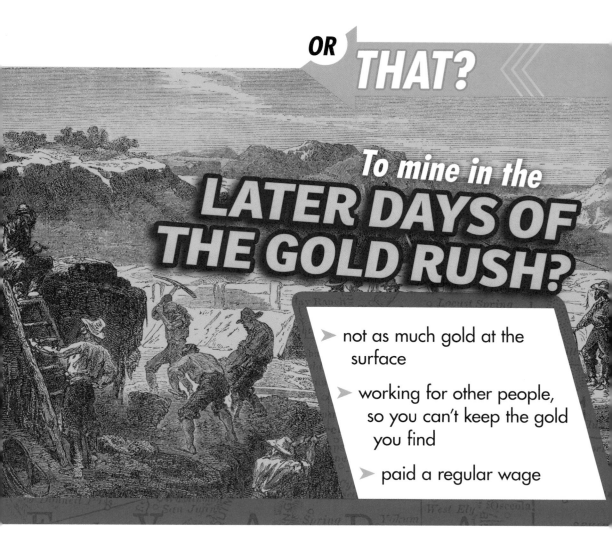

To mine in the **LATER DAYS OF THE GOLD RUSH?**

➤ not as much gold at the surface

➤ working for other people, so you can't keep the gold you find

➤ paid a regular wage

As the gold rush wore on, surface gold became harder to find. There was more gold deep underground, but individual miners didn't have the tools to dig it up. Many miners joined large mining companies. These companies paid miners to work in gold mines. Miners could no longer "strike it rich" by keeping the gold they found. But they had a steadier source of money.

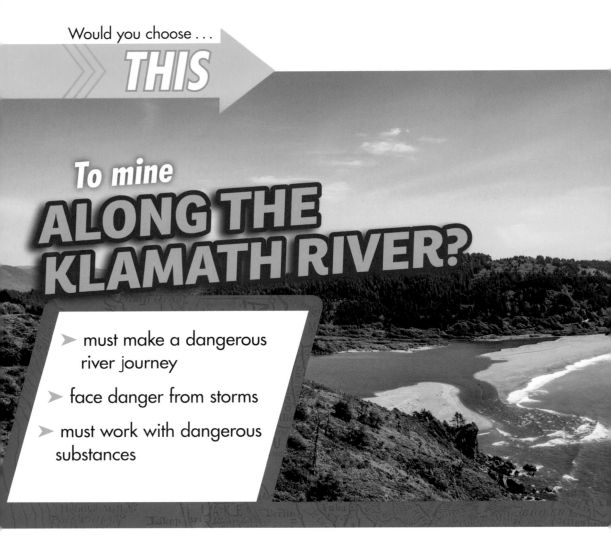

Would you choose . . .

THIS

To mine
ALONG THE KLAMATH RIVER?

- must make a dangerous river journey
- face danger from storms
- must work with dangerous substances

The Klamath River is north of San Francisco. Miners traveled there by boat, which meant facing storms and choppy waters. Storms caused sand at the bottom of the river to shift and build up. Miners sometimes had to abandon boats that got stuck. The gold along Klamath River was in heavy black sand. Miners used quicksilver, or **mercury**, to separate it. Mercury is **toxic**. Overexposure can cause people to throw up and feel weak.

ON EUREKA PEAK?

To mine

> weather changes quickly

> danger of falling

> harsh winters

Eureka Peak is a mountain northeast of San Francisco. Miners there mined gold from high mountain cliffs. They were in danger of injuring themselves in falls. Miners also had to watch the weather, which could change quickly. Winters on Eureka Peak were very cold and snowy. Miners couldn't mine if too much snow fell.

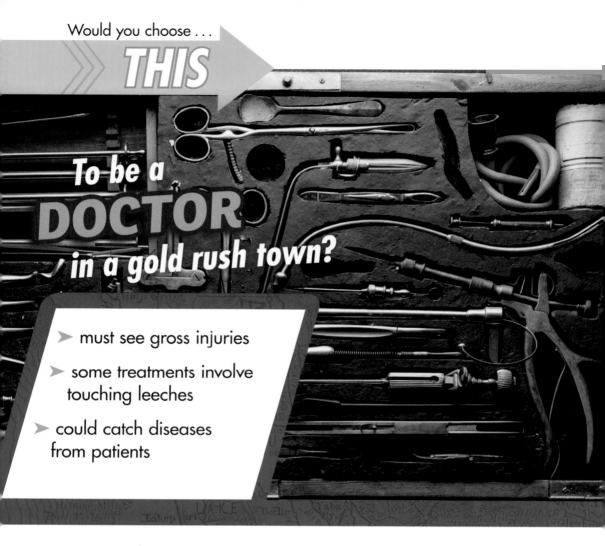

THIS

To be a DOCTOR in a gold rush town?

- ➤ must see gross injuries
- ➤ some treatments involve touching leeches
- ➤ could catch diseases from patients

Gold rush doctors saw blood and gross injuries during surgeries and treatments. One common treatment at the time was making patients bleed on purpose. To do this, doctors might put bloodsucking worms called leeches on a patient's skin. Patients also coughed, sneezed, and puked near doctors often. Doctors were always at risk from catching diseases from patients.

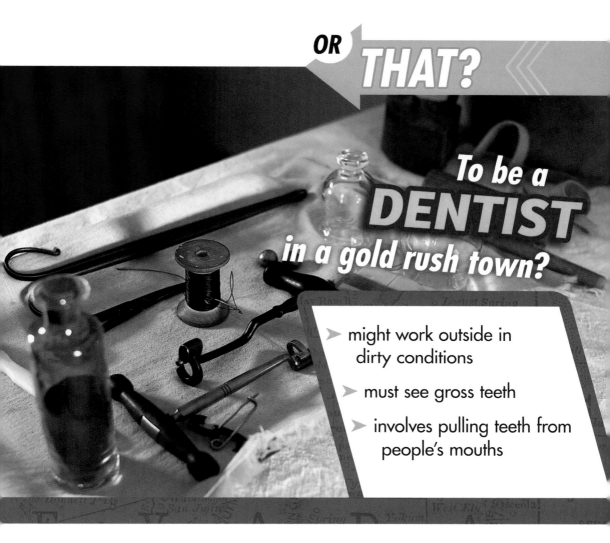

To be a
DENTIST
in a gold rush town?

➤ might work outside in dirty conditions

➤ must see gross teeth

➤ involves pulling teeth from people's mouths

Gold rush dentists worked in dirty conditions. A dentist's "office" could be a barrel with a stick attached for a headrest. Miners would rinse with water from a cup and spit on the ground near the dentist's feet. Some miners suffered from loose or rotting teeth. Dentists would have to work on and pull many gross teeth.

Would you choose . . .

THIS

To
USE A PAN
to mine gold?

➤ simple process you can do yourself

➤ slow process

➤ likely to find less gold than from other methods

Some miners panned for gold. A pan looks like a shallow bowl. Miners swirled river **sediment** and water in it. This separated heavy gold nuggets and gold dust. A miner who panned kept whatever gold he found. But the process was slow. On a good day, a miner sifted through about four pans of sediment an hour. It was rare to find large gold nuggets using pans. Usually, miners only collected gold dust.

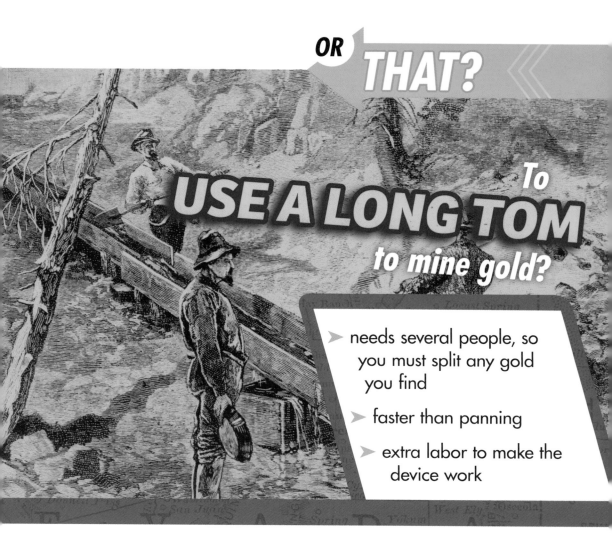

To USE A LONG TOM to mine gold?

➤ needs several people, so you must split any gold you find

➤ faster than panning

➤ extra labor to make the device work

A Long Tom is a metal **trough**. Miners shoveled dirt into it. Water carried the dirt over grooves that separated gold and sand. A Long Tom took at least three miners to operate. But it was faster than panning. The Long Tom needed to be near fast-moving water to work. Miners who couldn't find room on a riverbank had to dig **trenches** to bring water closer to the device.

Would you choose . . .

THIS

To face the FLOOD IN SACRAMENTO in 1849 and 1850?

- ➤ must wait for water to go down
- ➤ can't mine
- ➤ buildings destroyed

From late 1849 into early 1850, a rainy winter caused a flood in the gold rush town of Sacramento. Many people were trapped in buildings as water rushed into the streets. It took 10 days for the water to go down. Some buildings were washed away completely. A miner's equipment could be washed away in flood waters.

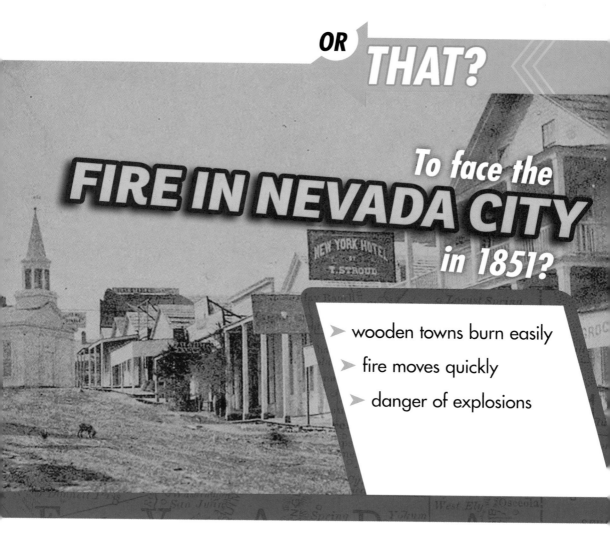

FIRE IN NEVADA CITY

To face the ... in 1851?

> wooden towns burn easily

> fire moves quickly

> danger of explosions

One night in 1851, a fire started in Nevada City. Buildings there were made of wood and **canvas**. They were packed tightly together. The fire moved quickly and was hard to put out. Many people lost their homes and belongings. The fire also sparked a barrel of blasting powder. This caused an explosion that made the fire worse.

THIS

To pay for a

HEALTHY MEAL?

➤ reminder of home

➤ better taste

➤ better protection against sickness

Most miners were not used to being away from home and cooking for themselves. They made easy, unhealthy meals such as flour **dumplings**. Some women living in gold rush towns made money selling food to miners. A healthy meal could protect against scurvy. A home-cooked meal could also lift a miner's spirits.

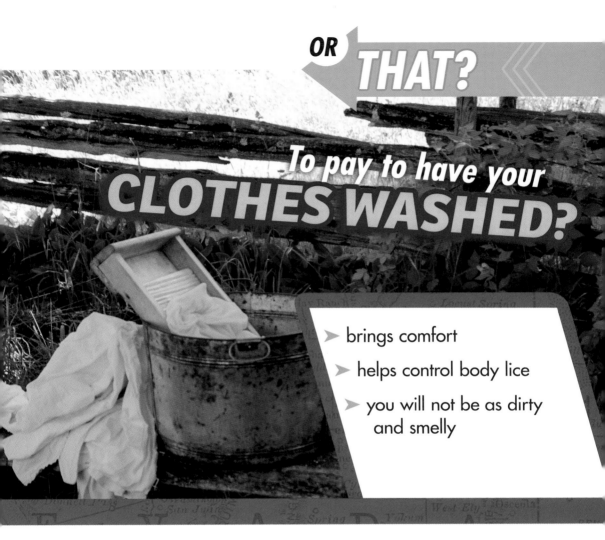

To pay to have your **CLOTHES WASHED?**

- ➤ brings comfort
- ➤ helps control body lice
- ➤ you will not be as dirty and smelly

Women in gold rush towns also made money by washing miners' clothes. Mining made clothes very dirty. Miners didn't take baths or wash their clothes very often. This put them at risk of getting body lice. These small bugs live in dirty clothes. They bite people and make them itch. Washing clothes helped control lice. It could also help miners feel more comfortable.

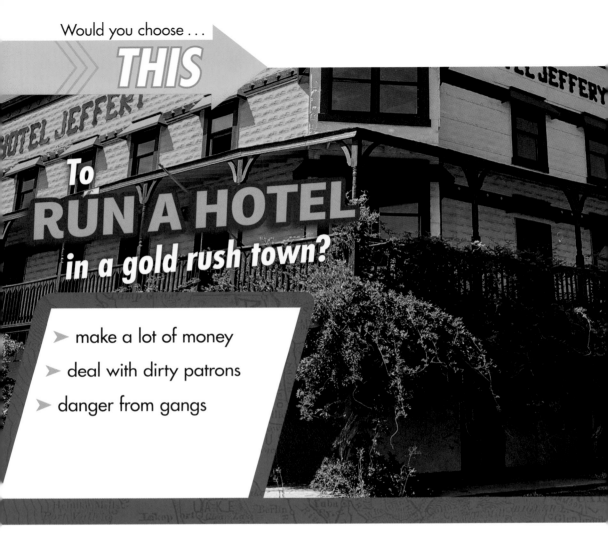

Would you choose . . .

THIS

To RUN A HOTEL
in a gold rush town?

➤ make a lot of money

➤ deal with dirty patrons

➤ danger from gangs

Hotel owners made lots of money housing miners. Hotels were smelly and crowded. The miners did not bathe often. Hotel owners might also have to deal with street gangs. These gangs made business owners pay for "protection." If an owner didn't pay, the gang members might burn down his or her business.

To
BE A FARMER
in a gold rush town?

> make a lot of money

> hydraulic mines can ruin crops

> constantly fighting with large mining companies

Farmers also made lots of money during the gold rush. The growing population needed a lot of food! However, farmers dealt with nearby **hydraulic** mines. These mines used water to blast gold out of rock. The water washed rocks, dirt, sand, and **silt** into farm fields. This ruined crops. Farmers constantly fought with mining companies to stop hydraulic mining.

THIS

To work in an
UNDERGROUND MINE?

- constantly around explosions
- work underground with little light
- face dangers that could lead to death

Large mining companies mined gold deep within mountains. Miners worked in tunnels to blast gold out of rock and cart it to the surface. Working underground was dirty and dangerous. The tunnels didn't get much light. They could also flood with water or collapse. Miners were constantly at risk of being trapped or dying.

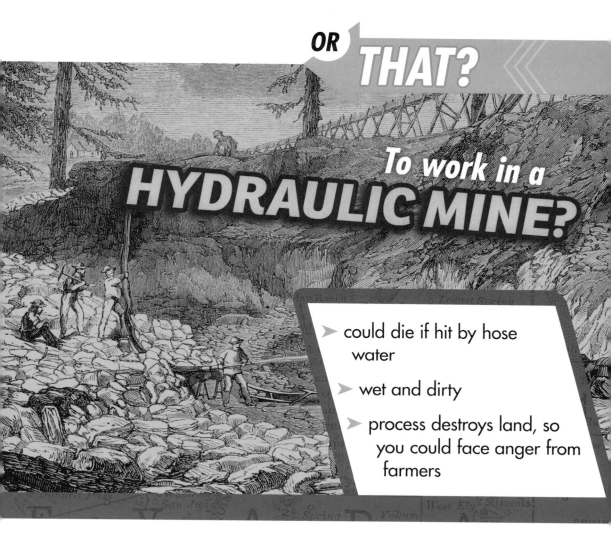

To work in a HYDRAULIC MINE?

> could die if hit by hose water

> wet and dirty

> process destroys land, so you could face anger from farmers

Hydraulic mining used a giant water hose to blast rock into pieces. A miner who got hit by the stream could die. Hydraulic mining was messy. Miners got covered in wet dirt. Hydraulic mining also flooded nearby farms with runoff. As a hydraulic miner, you could face anger from local farmers.

Would you choose . . .

THIS

To STAY IN CALIFORNIA
after failing to strike it rich in the gold rush?

➤ might never see some of your family back east

➤ have to find new job

➤ opportunity to start a new life in a promising area

Some miners chose to start new lives in California after failing to get rich. This meant working for wages in a mine or finding a new job. It could also mean leaving behind family back east forever. But it also offered new opportunities. Mining towns grew into established towns with better jobs. Some former miners became farmers, ranchers, and business owners.

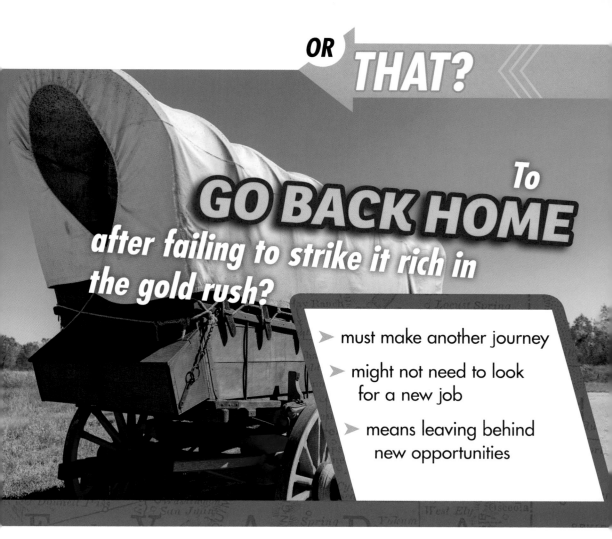

To
GO BACK HOME
after failing to strike it rich in the gold rush?

> must make another journey

> might not need to look for a new job

> means leaving behind new opportunities

Other miners returned home after striking out in the gold rush. This meant making another exhausting journey, which could take months. Some people had their old jobs and lives waiting for them. They didn't have to look for new work. However, they left behind new opportunities in the growing state of California.

LIGHTNING ROUND

Would you choose to . . .

➤ eat stewed beans or flour dumplings for an entire week?

➤ see a play or go bowling for Sunday-night entertainment in a gold rush town?

➤ use the last of your money to buy boots or better mining equipment?

➤ have fleas on your body or lice in your hair?

➤ crush a finger while mining or lose a tooth to scurvy?

➤ have the job of shoveling dirt into a Long Tom or removing large rocks from it?

➤ buy a stamp to send a letter home or buy an old newspaper to get news from back east?

➤ eat oysters or fried deer tongue during a holiday celebration?

bacterium (bak-TEER-ee-uhm)—a microscopic, single-celled living thing that can be useful or harmful

canvas (KAN-vuhs)—a type of course, strong cloth

diarrhea (dye-uh-REE-uh)—a condition in which normally solid waste from your body becomes liquid

dumpling (DUHMP-ling)—dough that has been boiled, fried, or steamed, sometimes with meat, vegetables, or fruit inside

hydraulic (hye-DRAW-lik)—working on power that is created by liquid moving through pipes or under pressure

mercury (MUR-kyur-ee)—a silvery metal that is poisonous and liquid at room temperature

pan (PAN)—to wash gravel in a pan to look for gold

rut (RUHT)—a deep, narrow track made in the ground from the repeated passage of wheels

sediment (SED-uh-muhnt)—rock, sand, or dirt that has been carried to a place by water, wind, or a glacier

silt (SILT)—fine particles of soil that are carried along by flowing water

toxic (TAHK-sic)—poisonous

trench (TRENCH)—a long, narrow ditch

trough (TRAWF)—a long, narrow container

vomit (VAH-mit)—to bring up food from the stomach and expel it through the mouth

READ MORE

Gregory, Josh. *If You Were a Kid During the California Gold Rush.* New York: Children's Press, an imprint of Scholastic Inc., 2018.

Katirgis, Jane. *Meet John Sutter: California Gold Rush Pioneer.* New York: Enslow Publishing, 2020.

Micklos, John. *A Primary Source History of the Gold Rush.* Mankato, MN: Capstone Press, 2016.

INTERNET SITES

DK Find Out—Gold
https://www.dkfindout.com/us/earth/rocks-and-minerals/gold/

Ducksters—Westward Expansion: California Gold Rush
https://www.ducksters.com/history/westward_expansion/california_gold_rush.php

Scholastic—Back to the Gold Rush?
http://www.scholastic.com/browse/article.jsp?id=3755940